Critical Thinking Activities

W9-ARW-213

Critical Thinking Activities

HELP STUDENTS:

- Reinforce Essential Chapter Skills
- Master Higher-Level Thinking Skills

McGraw Hill Glencoe

TO THE TEACHER

Critical Thinking Activities *complements the critical thinking skills introduced in the textbook. Each reproducible skill activity is designed to increase student understanding and application of the skill introduced in the text by providing additional practice.*

The skill activity begins with an introduction that reviews the key information necessary to students' understanding. The introduction is followed by directions, the application, and questions. Answers are provided in the back of this booklet.

CREATING A CUSTOMIZED FILE

The individual booklets in the **Teacher's Classroom Resources** *provide a wide variety of supplemental materials to help make economics meaningful to students. These resources appear as individual booklets in a carryall file box.*

There are a variety of ways to organize your classroom resources. Three alternatives are given here:

■ **Organize by category** (all activities, all tests, etc.)

■ **Organize by category and chapter** (all Chapter 1 activities, all Chapter 1 tests, etc.)

■ **Organize sequentially by lesson** (activities, quizzes, and other materials for Chapter 1, Section I; Chapter 1, Section 2, etc.)

Regardless of the organization you choose, you may pull out individual activity sheets from these booklets, or you may photocopy them directly from the booklets and file the photocopies. You will then be able to keep original booklets intact in a safe place.

The McGraw·Hill Companies

 Glencoe

Copyright © by The McGraw-Hill Companies, Inc. All rights reserved. Permission is granted to reproduce the material contained herein on the condition that such materials be reproduced only for classroom use; be provided to students, teachers, and families without charge; and be used solely in conjunction with the *Economics: Principles and Practices* and *Economics: Today and Tomorrow* programs. Any other reproduction, for sale or other use, is expressly prohibited.

Send all inquiries to:
Glencoe/McGraw-Hill
8787 Orion Place
Columbus, OH 43240-4027

ISBN: 978-0-07-895342-2
MHID: 0-07-895342-1

Printed in the United States of America.

2 3 4 5 6 7 8 9 10 WDQ 13 12 11 10

CONTENTS

CRITICAL THINKING 1

WHAT IS THE MAIN IDEA?

When finding the main idea in a passage, you should organize the information given and then assess the most important concept to remember. The excerpt below, for example, is from the introduction to economist Robert Heilbroner's 1953 book The Worldly Philosophers.

Directions: To determine the main idea, read the excerpt below and then answer the questions that follow.

By all rules of [the] history books, they were nonentities: they commanded no armies, sent no men to their deaths, ruled no empires, took little part in history-making decisions. . . . Yet what they did was more decisive for history than many acts of statesmen who basked in brighter glory, often more profoundly disturbing than the shuttling of armies back and forth across frontiers, more powerful for good and bad than the edicts of kings and legislatures. It was this: they shaped and swayed men's minds.

And because he who enlists a man's mind wields a power even greater than the sword or the scepter, these men shaped and swayed the world. Few of them ever lifted a finger in action. . . . But they left in their train shattered empires and exploded continents, they buttressed and undermined regimes, they set class against class and even nation against nation—not because they plotted mischief, but because of the extraordinary power of their ideas.

. . . A man who thinks that economics is only a matter for professors forgets that this is the science that has sent men to the barricades. . . . No, the great economists pursued an inquiry as exciting—and dangerous—as any the world has ever known. . . . The notions of the great economists were world-shaking, and their mistakes nothing short of calamitous.

1. Who wrote this excerpt?

_____

2. What is the purpose of the reading from which the excerpt is taken?

_____

_____

3. What is the general subject of the excerpt?

_____

4. Underline the sentence that best sums up the main idea of the excerpt.

5. Restate at least three additional details from the excerpt that support the main idea.

_____

_____

_____

Copyright © by The McGraw-Hill Companies, Inc.

CRITICAL THINKING 2

CAUSE AND EFFECT IN A MARKET ECONOMY

When identifying cause and effect, you first look for a cause, or something that makes some-thing else happen. Then you look for the effect, or the result of the cause. For example, mixed economies like the one in the United States involve many cause-and-effect relationships.

Directions: *Read all the following statements to identify the cause or effect in each relationship diagrammed below. Then write the letter of each statement in the correct place in the appropriate diagram.*

Example:

A. Few people buy the Head Bangers' first CD.

B. The music company refuses to sign the Head Bangers for a second CD.

Cause		Effect
A	→	B

C. Businesses produce goods that people want at a price that people will pay.

D. A poll reports that consumers want to take pictures with their cell phones.

E. No single company can control the price of a particular service or product.

F. Factors of production are wasted.

G. Businesses keep their production costs as low as possible.

H. A large number of independent sellers offer a product or service.

I. A person may practice medicine in the United States.

J. Fewer goods and services overall are produced.

K. Americans want their economic system to be fair and just.

L. Consumers experience a shortage of goods.

M. Americans want protection against risks beyond their control.

N. Voters elect lawmakers that support laws dealing with issues such as a minimum wage for unskilled workers.

O. A person passes through an approved medical school and receives a license from a state government.

P. A company that produces cell phones adds a camera feature to its product.

Q. The United States government offers programs such as unemployment compensation and Medicare.

Cause	Effect		Cause	Effect		Cause	Effect
O →	____		____ →	J		G →	____

Cause	Effect		Cause	Effect		Cause	Effect
H →	____		J →	____		____ →	N

Cause	Effect		Cause	Effect
____ →	Q		D →	____

Critical Thinking Activities

Copyright © by The McGraw-Hill Companies, Inc.

CRITICAL THINKING 3

CATEGORIZING INFORMATION ABOUT BUSINESS ORGANIZATIONS

Categorizing helps you deal with many facts in an organized way. For example, the advantages and disadvantages of business organizations can be studied by organizing facts in a chart.

Directions: Categorize the information about two types of business organizations by writing the number of each phrase below in the correct space or spaces.

Business Organization	Advantage	Disadvantage
Sole Proprietorship		
Partnership		

1. usually limited capital
2. ease of starting up
3. ease of management
4. only one special IRS schedule required at tax time
5. establishment involves only fees for attorney and state
6. potential for conflict
7. enjoyment of profits without having to share them
8. no separate business income tax preparation
9. more easily attracts top talent
10. satisfaction of being your own boss
11. ease of getting out of business
12. attracts financial capital more easily
13. personal and full responsibility for all business losses and debts
14. difficulty raising financial capital
15. each responsible for acts of all other partners
16. often limited managerial experience
17. difficult attracting qualified employees
18. limited life
19. more efficient operations because of larger size
20. less efficient operations because of size

Copyright © by The McGraw-Hill Companies, Inc.

CRITICAL THINKING 4

Making PREDICTIONS ABOUT CONSUMER DEMAND

Predicting future events is difficult, but the study of consumer demand makes predictions less risky.

Directions: *Use your knowledge of consumer demand to complete each prediction below. Circle the choice that you think an economist would approve.*

1. A hair dye is successfully advertised in the media.

   Prediction: Its demand curve will shift (right, left, up, down).

2. People get tired of iPods™.

   Prediction: The demand curve for iPods™ will shift (right, left, up, down).

3. The price of butter goes up.

   Prediction: The demand for margarine will (increase, stay the same, decrease).

4. The prices of computers go down.

   Prediction: People will buy (more, the same amount of, less) software.

5. The price of insulin goes down.

   Prediction: Diabetics will use (more, the same amount, less).

6. The price of salt doubles.

   Prediction: Shoppers will buy (more, the same amount, less).

7. The price of new automobiles goes up.

   Prediction: The demand for used cars will (rise, remain the same, fall).

8. Strawberries are in season.

   Prediction: The demand for frozen strawberries will (rise, remain the same, fall).

9. The cost of casting materials triples.

   Prediction: A (smaller, similar, higher) ratio of patients with broken bones will get casts.

10. The price of beef falls.

    Prediction: People will buy (more, the same amount of, less) beef.

Copyright © by The McGraw-Hill Companies, Inc.

CRITICAL THINKING 5

MAKING GENERALIZATIONS ABOUT THE SUPPLY OF HOGS

Generalizations are judgments that are usually true, based on the facts at hand.

Directions: *Combine the facts in the following table with what you have read about the law of supply. Then answer the questions and choose the most likely generalizations below.*

U.S. Hog Production and Prices
(in thousands)

Year	Production	Price per Hog
1980	67,318	$38.00
1990	53,788	$53.70
1992	57,649	$41.60
1994	57,904	$39.90
1996	57,150	$51.90
1998	61,600	$81.00

1. What is the law of supply?

_____

2. A sure sign that the law of supply is prevailing is when production and prices are up. In which year on the table does it appear that the law of supply is prevailing? _____

3. How does the production of hogs differ from the production of a product that can be made in a matter of hours?

_____

_____

4. Based on your answer to question 3, when would you most likely see a decrease in the rate of hog production?

_____

5. When would you expect an increase in the rate of hog production?

_____

6. Did the production of hogs increase or decrease between 1980 and 1990? By how much?

_____

_____

7. Circle the letter of the generalization that is best supported by facts in the table.

   a. Farmers offer more hogs for sale when the price per hog is high.

   b. Farmers increase the production of hogs for sale after the price per hog goes up.

Copyright © by The McGraw-Hill Companies, Inc.

CRITICAL THINKING 6

COMPARING RATIONING AND THE PRICE SYSTEM

Making comparisons is an important skill because it helps you choose among alternatives. For example, economists have compared the allocation systems of price and rationing to find out which system has fewer difficulties.

Directions: Make your own comparison of price and rationing as systems to allocate scarce resources. Use the phrases below to complete the chart.

PRICE	RATIONING

Favors neither the producer nor the consumer

Entails decision-making for fair allocation

Accommodates change from natural disasters to war

Requires high administrative costs

Diminishes people's incentive to work for a larger allocation

Has no cost of administration

Understood well enough to allow people to make decisions quickly and efficiently

Encourages people to use their allocation carelessly

Based on the information in the chart, which system do you think economists might prefer? Explain your answer.

_____

_____

_____

Copyright © by The McGraw-Hill Companies, Inc.

CRITICAL THINKING 7

SUMMING UP CRITICISM OF OLIGOPOLISTS

Summarizing information means reducing a long reading to its main ideas and important facts. The following passage is from a 1912 presidential campaign speech of Woodrow Wilson. In the speech, he attacked the American oligopolies of the early 1900s.

Directions: *Read the following passage and write a summary of it on the lines below.*

American industry is not free, as it once was free; American enterprise is not free; the man with only a little capital is finding it harder to get into the field, more and more impossible to compete with the big fellow. Why? Because the laws of this country do not prevent the strong from crushing the weak. That is the reason, and because the strong have crushed the weak the strong dominate the industry and the economic life of this country. No man can deny that the lines of endeavor have more and more narrowed and stiffened; no man who knows anything about the development of industry in this country can have failed to observe that the larger kinds of credit are more and more difficult to obtain, unless you obtain them upon the terms of uniting your efforts with those who already control the industries of the country; and no one can fail to observe that any man who tries to set himself up in competition with any process of manufacture which has been taken under the control of large combinations of capital will presently find himself either squeezed out or obliged to sell and allow himself to be absorbed.

_____

_____

_____

_____

_____

_____

_____

_____

_____

_____

_____

_____

_____

_____

_____

_____

_____

_____

Copyright © by The McGraw-Hill Companies, Inc.

CRITICAL THINKING 8

Ⓢ YNTHESIZING THE GENDER PAY GAP

Synthesizing information involves combining information from two or more sources.

Directions: Use the figures in the first two tables to synthesize a third table that shows the mean (average) earnings of women as a percentage of the mean earnings of men in different age groups. Calculate the percentages and round to the nearest tenth.

Mean Earnings of Males, 2008	
Age Group	**Mean Earnings**
18 to 24	$28,246
25 to 34	$48,749
35 to 44	$65,839
45 to 54	$70,869
55 to 64	$72,773
65 and over	$69,489

Source: U.S. Census Bureau.

Mean Earnings of Females, 2008	
Age Group	**Mean Earnings**
18 to 24	$26,391
25 to 34	$39,037
35 to 44	$46,595
45 to 54	$45,984
55 to 64	$47,087
65 and over	$43,392

Source: U.S. Census Bureau.

The Gender Pay Gap, 2008	
Age Group	**Female Mean Earnings as a Percentage of Male Mean Earnings**

The gender pay gap is the largest in which age group? _____

Critical Thinking Activities

Copyright © by The McGraw-Hill Companies, Inc.

CRITICAL THINKING 9

FACTS AND OPINIONS ABOUT CONSUMER ISSUES

Distinguishing fact from opinion can help you make reasonable choices as a consumer. Read the following statements from ads. Label each one that states a fact with an F. Label each one that expresses an opinion with an O.

_____ **1.** You can buy autumn's best pumpkins at the World Market.

_____ **2.** The movie is a masterpiece, surely the best film of the year.

_____ **3.** R & F Antiques presents its annual fall show and sale this Saturday.

_____ **4.** Webzoom offers a monthly rate of $8 for unlimited Internet access!

_____ **5.** WashOMart offers free delivery on all washers and dryers over $390.

_____ **6.** Nissan pays your sales tax on all new Maxima leases.

_____ **7.** You get 20% off all purchases on the day you open a new account.

_____ **8.** We have the perfect dress, at the perfect price, for your perfect special occasion!

_____ **9.** You get the good life at a great price at Star.

_____ **10.** We are the only store in town to sell cashmere coats with Russian sable trim.

_____ **11.** At deVito's, you are guaranteed the lowest prices of the season.

_____ **12.** Buy 2, get 1 free.

_____ **13.** Larsen's is the greatest office supply store in Millville.

_____ **14.** We are the country's finest source for window and door replacement.

_____ **15.** We offer zero financing for 12 months.

_____ **16.** We have helped over 25,000 patients achieve their weight-loss goals.

_____ **17.** Selling on the Internet has never been so easy!

_____ **18.** This view is one you'll long remember.

_____ **19.** *The Magic Flute* is the most beautiful opera in the world.

_____ **20.** Hiller's hiking boots are more reliable than any other brand.

_____ **21.** Two very enthusiastic thumbs up!

_____ **22.** A house isn't comfortable unless its temperature is at least 68 degrees.

_____ **23.** Europe: There's a beautiful memory around every corner.

_____ **24.** Acetaminophen is less harmful to the stomach than aspirin is.

_____ **25.** Quebec: You'll want to come back again.

Copyright © by The McGraw-Hill Companies, Inc.

CRITICAL THINKING 10

CATEGORIZING CONSUMER CREDIT PROTECTION

Categorizing information can help when you have a credit problem. The items below are problems consumers face when using credit.

Directions: *On the following chart, write the number of the problem next to the government regulation that covers the situation.*

Major Federal Laws Regulating Consumer Credit		
Name of Law	**Main Purpose**	**Credit Problem**
Truth in Lending Act (1968)	Ensures that consumers are fully informed about the costs and conditions of borrowing	
Fair Credit Reporting Act (1970)	Protects the privacy and accuracy of information in a credit check	
Equal Credit Opportunity Act (1975)	Prohibits discrimination in giving credit on the basis of sex, race, religion, marital status, age, or receipt of public assistance	
Fair Credit Billing Act (1974)	Sets up a procedure for the quick correction of mistakes that appear on consumer credit accounts	
Fair Debt Collection Practices Act (1977)	Prevents abuse by professional debt collectors; does not apply to banks or other businesses that collect their own accounts	

1. Beth's latest billing statement shows an error of $100, and Beth wants the credit company to correct it.

2. A collection agency repeatedly calls Bob at work to ask when he will make his overdue car payments.

3. The bank refuses to loan Jane money, so she asks the bank representative for the name of the credit bureau that issued her credit report.

4. Jamal refuses to give his national origin on a loan application for an automobile.

5. Tim's credit card company raised the annual percentage rate on its cards without notifying its customers.

Copyright © by The McGraw-Hill Companies, Inc.

CRITICAL THINKING 11

COMPARISON SHOPPING FOR FOOD

Help Martin choose among alternatives. He has an upcoming dinner party for four. He would like to serve a cold drink with dinner, a meat or fish course, pasta, vegetable, and a dessert with coffee. He is using newspaper ads to plan his shopping list. He is short of time, and can shop at only one of the two stores listed below. Both stores offer the same products at the same prices, except for the sale items in the ads.

Directions: *Put together a dinner for Martin and his friends, spending no more than $15 and using only the products listed.*

Food Mart	Grocery Store
Macaroni & Cheese 4 boxes for $1.00 One for $.50	1 Gallon Mullins' Ice Cream $3.50 Regularly $4.79
Eight-inch Apple Pie $3.99 Regularly $7.00 ea.	Whole Beef Rib Eye $6.99 lb Regularly $8.99 lb.
One-serving Prepackaged Salad $1.99 Regularly $2.59 ea.	Cut Green Beans 3 cans for $2.00 One Can for $.75 a can
33-ounce Can of Coffee $5.99 Regularly $7.00 ea.	11-ounce Can of Coffee 3/$7.00 One Can for $3.50
Catfish $1.99 a pound Regularly $3.99 lb.	12-pack of Cola $2.50 Regularly $3.50

1. Shopping List at (name of store): _____

	Food	Quantity	Cost
2.	Cold Drink		
3.	Meat or Fish		
4.	Pasta		
5.	Vegetable		
6.	Coffee		
7.	Dessert		

8. Total cost: _____

9. Money saved by buying sale items: _____

Copyright © by The McGraw-Hill Companies, Inc.

CRITICAL THINKING 12

Sequencing Economic Development

The following are descriptions of different stages in economic development. Sequencing these examples, or information on any broad subject, will help you understand the material.

Directions: *Sequence the steps of economic development for an imaginary country by writing each letter in the appropriate development stage in the graphic organizer.*

a. The country begins to experience rapid growth as customs are put aside. The people seek new ways to do things and different techniques are introduced by other countries.

b. The country begins to move toward economic and cultural change, but does not yet experience economic growth.

c. The people in this country have most of their basic needs and wants met.

d. The makeup of the country's economy changes, with the national income growing faster than the population.

e. The country has no monetary system and may not be economically motivated to change.

f. The core of the country's industry is built at this time.

g. A formal economic organization does not exist in this society.

h. The country begins to save and invest more of its national income.

i. The emphasis changes from industrial production to providing services and public goods.

High Development:

Semidevelopment:

Takeoff:

Transition:

Primitive Equilibrium:

Copyright © by The McGraw-Hill Companies, Inc.

CRITICAL THINKING 13

MAKING INFERENCES ABOUT SAMUEL GOMPERS

When you make inferences, you use stated facts and information, as well as what you already know, to form ideas.

Directions: *Read the following information about the life of Samuel Gompers, a leader in the labor movement. Then answer the questions that follow.*

Samuel Gompers was born in London, England, in 1850. He went to school for only four years. When he left school, he received training as a cigar maker in London, and he began working at this trade as a young boy. Gompers and his family came to the United States in 1863. Eventually he, like many other immigrants, became active in labor unions.

In 1886 Gompers's views were more conservative than those of some other early labor leaders, who believed that strikes were acceptable. Gompers thought that laborers could achieve their goals by bargaining peacefully with business leaders and by voting for political candidates whose views were favorable to workers.

1. Was Gompers a skilled or an unskilled laborer? What information enables you to make this inference?

_____

_____

2. Do you infer that Gompers's parents were wealthy or not wealthy? What evidence helps you make this inference?

_____

_____

_____

3. Why might immigrants be especially attracted to labor unions?

_____

_____

4. Suppose the workers at a factory have not received a pay raise in five years. In Gompers's view, which of the following actions would probably be the best way for the workers to try to obtain a raise quickly? Explain your choice.

  a. striking to compel management to grant a raise
  b. meeting with the factory owner to try to work things out
  c. voting for a presidential candidate who wants to help workers

_____

_____

_____

Copyright © by The McGraw-Hill Companies, Inc.

CRITICAL THINKING 14

SYNTHESIZING FIGURES FOR CHANGE IN GOVERNMENT REVENUES

Synthesizing information involves integrating facts.

Directions: *Use the information in the table below to help understand how the government's sources of income changed between 2008 and 2010.*

U.S. Budget Receipts

(in Billions of Dollars)

Source	2008	2010	% Change
Individual income taxes	$1,146	$1,051	
Corporation income taxes	$304	$179	
Social insurance taxes	$900	$940	
Excise taxes	$67	$75	
Estate and gift taxes	$29	$20	
All other receipts	$78	$67	
Total Budget Receipts			

1. Calculate the percentage of change for each revenue source. Use your answers to complete the above table. (To find the percentage of change between 2008 and 2010, divide the difference by the amount for 2008.)

2. The amount of which source of revenue changed least between 2008 and 2010?

_____

3. What were the federal government's total budget receipts in 2008? 2010?

_____

4. What is the percentage change in total receipts between 2008 and 2010? _____

5. The amount of revenue from which two sources decreased by the largest percentages from 2008 to 2010?

_____

6. Based on the new information you have calculated and your knowledge of the economy, what is one conclusion that you can draw?

_____

Copyright © by The McGraw-Hill Companies, Inc.

CRITICAL THINKING 15

BIAS AND GOVERNMENT SPENDING

In the town of Lakeside, a large parcel of land on Raccoon Lake is for sale. One group of citizens wants the town government to buy the land and turn it into a nature preserve. Another group wants to make the land available for houses. The following two letters, each advocating a different point of view, were sent to the Lakeside Weekly News.

Directions: *Read the letters and look for signs of bias, and then answer the questions that follow.*

Letter 1

To the Editor: The population of Lakeside is growing. Young families are desperate for housing. Depending on how it is subdivided, this land could provide homes for ten to fifteen families. People have a right to have houses on the lake, so that they can enjoy the wholesome sports of swimming and boating. Only tree huggers and nature extremists object to building houses here. And if the town buys the land, our taxes will go up outrageously.

Letter 2

To the Editor: We, as a community, need to preserve this place of natural beauty for future generations. The land along Raccoon Lake is home to many wildflowers and animals. Every year, hundreds of hikers, birdwatchers, and other people use this land for recreation. If houses are built on that land, it will become ugly and barren. Turning this natural paradise into a housing development would be a tragic loss for Lakeside.

1. Identify the statements of fact in each letter.

   _____

   _____

2. Writers often show their bias by using emotional language. Identify examples of emotional language in each letter.

   _____

   _____

3. A person's bias is affected by his or her background, including such things as occupation, family and financial situation, and hobbies. What are some specific factors that might affect the point of view of each of the letter writers?

   _____

   _____

   _____

4. On a separate sheet of paper, list questions that you might ask each letter writer to help yourself evaluate his or her point of view.

Copyright © by The McGraw-Hill Companies, Inc.

CRITICAL THINKING 16

PRIMARY AND SECONDARY SOURCES ON FORMS OF MONEY

Primary sources are records of events by people who witnessed them. Secondary sources pull together information and provide an overview of events after they occur.

Directions: *In the space before each of the following passages, write P if it is a primary source or S if it is a secondary source. Then after each secondary source, write the number of the primary source that supports it in the box provided.*

_____ **1.** By the beginning of 1780 Congress had issued $191,500,000 in paper money ("Continentals"). . . An attempt had been made to retire some of the paper money, but when the failure of states to provide for the current expenses of the war resulted in exceeding the amount retired by over $35 million Continental currency dropped precipitately. *Encyclopedia of American History*, Sixth Edition ☐

_____ **2.** The other revenue, you see, was just salary obtained for regular work; but here was a little business operation upon my own account, and I was very proud indeed of my gold dollar every week."How I Served My Apprenticeship," by Andrew Carnegie, *The Youth's Companion*, April 23, 1896. ☐

_____ **3.** Barter requires a double coincidence of wants. Each party to a transaction must want exactly what the other person has to offer. In the past, bartering was used extensively, both within and between societies. Today, however, bartering works only in small societies with fairly simple economic systems. Glencoe's *Economics Today and Tomorrow* ☐

_____ **4.** They afterwards came to the ship's boats where we were, swimming and bringing us parrots, cotton threads in skeins, darts, and many other things; and we exchanged them for other things that we gave them, such as glass beads and copper bells. From *The Journal of Christopher Columbus* ☐

_____ **5.** Such also, at the beginning of the War of Independence, was the state of want of the insurgent army, and such was the scarcity of money, and the poverty of that government, now so rich, powerful, and prosperous, that its notes, called Continental paper money, were nearly valueless. By the Chevalier de Pontgibaud, *A French Volunteer of the War of Independence* ☐

_____ **6.** Coming to Pittsburgh from Scotland at the age of 13, Carnegie went to work in a cotton factory, where he earned $1.20 for working a 72-hour week. *History of a Free Nation* ☐

Copyright © by The McGraw-Hill Companies, Inc.

CRITICAL THINKING 17

STOCKS AND STOCKHOLDERS: WHAT'S THE IDEA?

Finding the main idea helps you to organize information and assess the most important concepts to remember.

Directions: *Read the following passage, then answer the questions below.*

Corporations are formed by selling shares of stock (also called securities). By issuing stock for sale, a company obtains funds for use in expanding its business. Shares of stock entitle the buyer to a certain part of the future profits and assets of the corporation selling the stock. The person buying stock, therefore, becomes a partial owner of the corporation. As proof of ownership, the corporation issues stock certificates.

   Stockholders, or owners of stock, benefit from stock in two ways. One is through dividends, the return a stockholder receives on the amount that he or she invested in the company. The corporation may declare a dividend at any time during a year. Dividends typically are paid only when the company makes a profit. The other way people benefit from stock is by selling it for more than they paid for it. Some people buy stock just to speculate, hoping that the price will increase greatly so they can sell it at a profit.

from *Economics Today and Tomorrow*

1. What is the general purpose of the passage?

_____

2. Sum up in a sentence the main idea, or most important concept, in the passage.

_____

_____

3. List at least five details from the passage that support the main idea.

_____

_____

_____

_____

_____

_____

Copyright © by The McGraw-Hill Companies, Inc.

CRITICAL THINKING 18

DRAWING CONCLUSIONS ABOUT THE ECONOMY

When you draw a conclusion, you interpret facts and make inferences about those facts.

Directions: *Study the following table. Then make inferences by answering the questions below. Use your inferences to draw a conclusion about the United States economy in 1999.*

OVERVIEW OF AMERICAN ECONOMY
measured by percent growth in gross domestic product, personal income, and disposable personal income during two quarters of 1998 and of 1999.

	1998		1999	
	Quarter 3	Quarter 4	Quarter 1	Quarter 2
Gross Domestic Product (GDP)	3.8	5.9	3.7	1.9
Personal income:				
New England	1.6	1.7	0.5	1.3
Mideast	1.2	0.7	2.2	1.0
Great Lakes	0.7	2.0	0.7	1.4
Plains	1.0	2.5	0.4	1.5
Southeast	1.5	1.4	0.9	1.1
Southwest	1.6	1.4	1.0	1.5
Rocky Mountains	1.3	2.2	1.3	1.2
Far West	1.5	1.8	1.8	1.3
Disposable personal income (DI) in the U.S. in "real" dollars	4.5	4.8	4.1	3.2

1. What seemed to be the relationship between the GDP and DI in the United States during the last half of 1998 and the first half of 1999?

_____

_____

2. Did any region(s) of the country experience an overall drop in personal income between 1998 and 1999? Explain your answer.

_____

_____

3. Which region experienced the greatest percentage of growth in personal income during 1998 and 1999? How do you know?

_____

4. What can you conclude about the condition of the United States economy in 1999 based on inferences made from the table?

_____

Copyright © by The McGraw-Hill Companies, Inc.

CRITICAL THINKING 19

CAUSES AND EFFECTS OF INFLATION

A cause is the action or situation that produces an event. An effect is what happens as a result of an event.

Directions: *Each item below is either a cause or an effect of inflation. (One item is both.) Copy each item in the correct column in the following chart.*

INFLATION

CAUSES	EFFECTS

1. Prices go up, the dollar buys less, and people on fixed incomes have decreased purchasing power.

2. Interest rates go up and spending on automobiles and houses falls.

3. Consumers, businesses, and governments try to buy more goods and services than the economy can produce.

4. The federal government spends more money than it collects in revenues.

5. The cost of labor goes up forcing manufacturers to raise prices.

6. People speculate heavily to take advantage of rising prices.

7. Loans are repaid in dollars that have less purchasing power because they buy less.

8. Higher prices force workers to ask for higher wages.

9. The Federal Reserve System increases the money supply faster than the increase in the Gross Domestic Product.

10. The cost of a raw material such as oil unexpectedly increases.

Copyright © by The McGraw-Hill Companies, Inc.

CRITICAL THINKING 20

Ⓕ ACTS AND OPINIONS ABOUT THE FEDERAL RESERVE SYSTEM

Facts can be proved by evidence such as records, documents, or historical sources. Opinions are based on people's differing values and beliefs.

Directions: *In the space before each of the following sentences, write F if the sentence states a fact or O if it states an opinion. In the spaces below, write an opinion related to two of the facts.*

_____ **1.** "The Federal Reserve cannot put a dollar in anyone's pocket, provide jobs for very many people, or buy more than a tiny amount of goods and services that the nation produces." *The Washington Post*, February 10, 1999

_____ **2.** Congress created the Federal Reserve System in 1913 as the central banking organization in the United States.

_____ **3.** The operations of the U.S. Federal Reserve System are downright mysterious.

_____ **4.** The Federal Reserve's policies have made money too tight in the United States.

_____ **5.** Credit is abundant in a country with an expansionary, or loose money, policy.

_____ **6.** If money becomes too plentiful, too quickly, prices increase and the purchasing power of the dollar decreases dramatically.

_____ **7.** The President appoints the members of the Fed's Board of Governors.

_____ **8.** Since 1913 the Fed has set specific reserve requirements for many banks.

_____ **9.** "Not too many years ago, Federal Reserve officials conducted monetary policy as if they were members of the Politburo plotting behind the thick walls of the Kremlin." *Business Week*, January 11, 1999

_____ **10.** "The remarkable surge in the availability of real-time information in recent years has sharply reduced the degree of uncertainty confronting business management." Alan Greenspan, commencement address at Harvard, 1999

Opinion 1:

_____

_____

Opinion 2:

_____

_____

Copyright © by The McGraw-Hill Companies, Inc.

CRITICAL THINKING 21

Sources on Economic Stability

Primary sources are original records of events. Secondary sources are documents created after an event occurred. They analyze and interpret events and information.

Directions: *Read the following excerpt from an article that was posted on the Web site of CNN (Cable News Network) on November 2, 1999. Then answer the questions that follow.*

U.S. consumer spending rose at a moderate pace in September while Hurricane Floyd flattened income levels by keeping thousands of East Coast workers temporarily away from their jobs, the government reported Tuesday.

Personal income was flat in September, compared to the 0.3 percent gain expected by analysts and the 0.4 percent rise recorded in August, the Commerce Department said. Without the effects of Hurricane Floyd, personal income would have risen 0.3 percent, the report said, in line with forecasts.

Consumer spending, meantime, advanced 0.4 percent, just above analysts' estimates of a 0.3 increase but half the 0.8 gain registered the month before. Consumer spending fuels about two-thirds of the nation's economy.

Even with the one-time weather-related effects, economists took the numbers as encouraging signs that consumer spending is beginning to slow, reducing the threat of accelerating inflation. . . .

1. Is the excerpt above a primary source or a secondary source, or does it combine aspects of both? Explain.

_____

_____

_____

2. What is the writer's *main* purpose: stating facts or expressing an opinion?

_____

3. What is the source that the writer cites? Is that source reliable?

_____

_____

4. Suppose you were a historian 100 years from now and you were analyzing economic stability in the 1990s. What are some kinds of additional information you would need?

_____

_____

_____

Copyright © by The McGraw-Hill Companies, Inc.

CRITICAL THINKING 22

Making Generalizations About International Trade

Generalizations are judgments based on the facts at hand. For a generalization to be valid, it must be based on facts.

Directions: *Read each of the following passages and pairs of generalizations. In the space before the valid generalization, write V. Then explain your choice on the lines below.*

1. Many Europeans are reluctant to consume genetically altered products such as corn and wheat that have superior yield, taste, and disease resistance. A more sensitive case is that of American beef raised on artificial hormones, a product that Europeans refuse to import. While most Americans feel that their food is safe, Europeans are not so sure. After all, they point out, a recent American experiment demonstrated that Monarch butterflies died when they ate the pollen from genetically altered corn plants.

   _____ The United States is not the only country to use health issues to restrict trade.

   _____ Many Europeans believe that food imported from the United States is unsafe.

   _____

   _____

2. Tariffs and quotas protect domestic jobs from cheap foreign labor. Workers in the shoe industry have protested the import of lower-cost Italian, Spanish, and Brazilian shoes, because low-cost imports can endanger American jobs. Garment workers have opposed the import of lower-cost Korean, Chinese, and Indian clothing. Steelworkers have blocked foreign-made cars from company parking lots to show their displeasure with the foreign-made steel used in producing cars.

   _____ American workers have demonstrated opposition to imported goods.

   _____ Trade barriers help save American jobs by giving American industries time to develop.

   _____

   _____

3. When inefficient industries are protected, the economy produces less and the standard of living goes down. Because of the unnecessarily high prices, people buy less of everything, including those goods produced by protected industries. If prices get too high, substitute products will be found so protected jobs will still be lost.

   _____ Protectionist measures provide only temporary protection for domestic jobs.

   _____ Profits reward the efficient and hard working.

   _____

   _____

Copyright © by The McGraw-Hill Companies, Inc.

CRITICAL THINKING 23

$\mathbf{D}$RAWING INFERENCES AND MAKING CONCLUSIONS ABOUT STABILIZATION POLICIES

To draw an inference means to come to a logical conclusion based on available information. Each statement below provides evidence about the speaker's approach to economic stabilization.

Directions: For each statement below, draw an inference about whether the speaker is most likely a supporter of demand-side or supply-side policies. On the line below each statement, write "demand-side" or "supply-side" to reflect your conclusion.

1. "Rising federal deficits are okay because they are a byproduct of efforts to stimulate the economy. When the economy recovers, increased tax revenues will repay the debt."

   _____

2. "Taxes should be cut. Workers will be more productive if they can keep more of what they make."

   _____

3. "If investment spending drops by $50 billion, then overall spending will probably decline by $100 billion."

   _____

4. "We should reduce welfare programs. Stimulating production will create jobs, so fewer people will need welfare."

   _____

5. "Ronald Reagan did the right thing when he deregulated the savings and loan industry."

   _____

6. "For the most part, changes in GDP can be traced to the instability of business spending."

   _____

7. "Government should get off the backs of business."

   _____

8. "When business spending declines, government should spend more to offset this decline."

   _____

9. "I favor unemployment insurance because it bolsters consumer spending during a recession."

   _____

10. "When economic stability is threatened, the government should step in to correct the situation."

    _____

Copyright © by The McGraw-Hill Companies, Inc.

CRITICAL THINKING 24

COMPARING FISH CONSUMPTION IN DEVELOPED AND DEVELOPING COUNTRIES

A bar graph is a good way to show comparisons.

Directions: *Read the following facts from a report issued by the Food and Agriculture Organization of the United Nations. Then complete the bar graph comparing the percentage of fish consumption in different parts of the world. Use the figures in brackets.*

"Worldwide men, women and children eat more fish than any other type of animal protein. It is estimated that between 15 and 20 [16.4] percent of all animal proteins come from aquatic animals. Fish is highly nutritious and serves as a valuable supplement in diets lacking essential vitamins and minerals."

From "Fisheries and Food Security"

"In general people in developing countries are much more dependent on fish as part of their daily diets than those living in the developed world. Figures for 1995 show that while fish provide slightly over 7 [7.4] percent of animal protein in North and Central America and more than 9 [9.2] percent in Europe, in Africa they provide over 17 [17.4] percent, in Asia over 26 [26.2], and in the low-income food-deficit countries (LIFDCs) . . . they provide nearly 22 [21.8] percent."

From "Fisheries and Food Security"

Fish as Percentage of Total Animal Protein Intake						
World						
Asia						
Africa						
Europe						
North and Central America						
LIFDCs						

0   5   10   15   20   25   30

How much more do people in low-income food-deficit countries depend on fish for protein than people in the world in general?

_____

Copyright © by The McGraw-Hill Companies, Inc.

CRITICAL THINKING 25

SEQUENCING GLOBAL INFORMATION IN THE NEWS

The following events show how we share a global environment. To help organize all that you read on this, or any subject with such a broad scope, it helps to sequence the information.

Directions: *Read the following information involving pollution in Kenya's Lake Victoria. Use the table to sequence the information, making inferences if necessary. The first entry has been provided for you.*

a. Starved for plankton, the fish become diseased and many die.

b. Building on the Kenyan model, an international conference looks at how to use satellite technology for pollution control and resource allocation in other parts of the world.

c. The lake serves as a major source of employment for some 30 million people.

d. An unidentified oversupply of nutrients promotes the rampant spread of water hyacinth, which deprive fish and plankton of oxygen and sunlight.

e. Fishermen leave their villages in search of jobs. The women and children stay behind, facing severe poverty, disease, and malnutrition. What remains of the fishing industry is all but destroyed when the European Union bans the importation of Kenyan fish.

f. In September of 1999, the World Bank provides $1.3 million to finance removal of the water hyacinth.

g. The Kenyan government seeks to protect the coffee, tea and tourism industries from the kinds of environmental factors that have destroyed the fish industry. In August of 1999, industry leaders are encouraged to attend a five-day environmental requirements seminar in Nairobi, sponsored by a Swiss-based firm.

h. In November of 1999, satellite remote-sensing technology identifies the nutrients that have been feeding the water hyacinth. The research helps cash-strapped countries take strategic action within their means: Kenya will plant trees, a natural filter, at the mouths of rivers that feed Lake Victoria.

1st	2nd	3rd	4th	5th	6th	7th	8th
c							

Copyright © by The McGraw-Hill Companies, Inc.

CRITICAL THINKING 26

SYNTHESIZING INFORMATION ABOUT COMPUTERS AROUND THE WORLD

Synthesizing information involves combining information from two or more sources.

Directions: Study the following tables. Use the figures in the table to synthesize a third table that shows the number of personal computers per thousand people in each country. List the name of the country with the highest ratio of computers to population first and the country with the lowest ratio last.

Countries with the Most Personal Computers

Country Name	Number of Personal Computers in 2000
United States	154,000,000
Japan	45,000,000
Germany	28,000,000
United Kingdom	26,000,000
France	21,000,000
Canada	14,700,000

Population in Countries with the Most Personal Computers
(rounded to the nearest 1,000)

Country Name	Population
United States	270,312,000
Japan	125,932,000
Germany	82,790,000
United Kingdom	58,970,000
France	58,805,000
Canada	30,675,000

Number of Computers Per 1,000 People in Countries with the Most Personal Computers

Country Name	Number of Computers per 1,000 People

Critical Thinking Activities

Copyright © by The McGraw-Hill Companies, Inc.

Activity 1

1. economist Robert Heilbroner

2. to introduce the book *The Worldly Philosophers*

3. the importance of economists

4. <u>The notions of the great economists were world-shaking, and their mistakes nothing short of calamitous.</u>

5. In students' answers, look for ideas from the following passages: *what they did was more decisive for history than many acts of statesmen; they shaped and swayed men's minds; because he who enlists a man's mind wields a power even greater than the sword or the scepter, these men shaped and swayed the world; they left in their train shattered empires and exploded continents, they buttressed and undermined regimes, they set class against class and even nation against nation; the extraordinary power of their ideas; the science that has sent men to the barricades*

Activity 2

Cause		Effect
O	→	I

Cause		Effect
H	→	E

Cause		Effect
M	→	Q

Cause		Effect
F	→	J

Cause		Effect
J	→	L

Cause		Effect
D	→	P

Cause		Effect
G	→	C

Cause		Effect
K	→	N

Activity 3

Business Organization	Advantage	Disadvantage
Sole Proprietorship	2, 3, 7, 8, 10, 11	1, 13, 14, 16, 17, 18, 20
Partnership	2, 3, 4, 5, 9, 12, 19	6, 15, 18

Copyright © by The McGraw-Hill Companies, Inc.

Activity 4

1. **Prediction:** Its demand curve will shift right.

2. **Prediction:** The demand curve for beanie babies will shift left.

3. **Prediction:** The demand for margarine will increase.

4. **Prediction:** People will buy more software.

5. **Prediction:** Diabetics will use the same amount.

6. **Prediction:** Shoppers will buy the same amount.

7. **Prediction:** The demand for used cars will rise.

8. **Prediction:** The demand for frozen strawberries will fall.

9. **Prediction:** A similar ratio of patients with broken bones will get casts.

10. **Prediction:** People will buy more beef.

Activity 5

1. Suppliers will normally offer more for sale at high prices and less for sale at lower prices.

2. 1998

3. Raising hogs takes months.

4. after the price per hog drops

5. after the price per hog goes up

6. decrease; by 13,530

7. b

Activity 6

PRICE	RATIONING
Favors neither the producer nor the consumer	Entails decision-making for fair allocation
Accommodates change from natural disasters to war	Requires high administrative costs
Has no cost of administration	Diminishes people's incentive to work for a larger allocation
Understood well enough to allow people to make decisions quickly and efficiently	Encourages people to use their allocation carelessly

Economists probably prefer the price system because it poses fewer difficulties than rationing.

Activity 7

Students' summaries will vary. The following is a sample response:

American business is no longer free because the country's laws do not protect smaller industries. Unless a person joins the "big guys," he or she cannot obtain the backing needed to start a business. Any person who tries to compete will fail or be absorbed into larger businesses.

Activity 8

The Gender Pay Gap, 2008	
Age Group	Female Mean Earnings as a Percentage of Male Mean Earnings
18 to 24	93.4%
25 to 34	80.1%
35 to 44	70.8%
45 to 54	64.9%
55 to 64	64.7%
65 and over	62.4%

Age group with largest gender pay gap: 55 to 64 years.

Copyright © by The McGraw-Hill Companies, Inc.

ANSWER KEY

Activity 9

1. O
2. O
3. F
4. F
5. F
6. F
7. F
8. O
9. O
10. F
11. F
12. F
13. O
14. O
15. F
16. F
17. O
18. O
19. O
20. O
21. O
22. O
23. O
24. F
25. O

Activity 10

Name of Law	Credit Problem
Truth in Lending Act	5
Fair Credit Reporting Act	3
Equal Credit Opportunity Act	4
Fair Credit Billing Act	1
Fair Debt Collection Practices Act	2

Copyright © by The McGraw-Hill Companies, Inc.

Activity 11

Answers will vary. The following responses are samples:

1. Shopping List at Grocery Store

Food	Quantity	Cost
2. Cold Drink	12-pack of cola	$2.50
3. Meat or Fish	One pound of catfish	$3.99
4. Pasta	A box of macaroni and cheese	$.50
5. Vegetable	One can of green beans	$.75
6. Coffee	One 11-ounce can of coffee	$3.50
7. Dessert	One gallon of Mullins' Ice Cream	$3.50

8. Total cost: $14.74

9. Money saved by buying sale items: $2.29

Activity 12

Primitive Equilibrium: e, g

Transition: b

Takeoff: a, h

Semidevelopment: d, f

High Development: c, i

Activity 13

1. Gompers was skilled, because he received training as a cigar maker.

2. Gompers's parents probably weren't wealthy. If they had been wealthy, he would have received more education and not have begun work as a young boy.

3. Immigrants were attracted to the labor-union movement because most immigrants could obtain only low-paying jobs, and workers who have low-paying jobs are especially interested in improving their working situation.

4. Gompers would probably advocate meeting with the factory owner. He did not support strikes. He did support political candidates who favored labor, but electing a presidential candidate would have little immediate impact on the wages of the workers in one factory.

Copyright © by The McGraw-Hill Companies, Inc.

Critical Thinking Activities

Activity 14

1.

U.S. Budget Receipts
(in Billions of Dollars)

Source	% Change
Individual income taxes	−8%
Corporation income taxes	−41%
Social insurance taxes	4%
Excise taxes	12%
Estate and gift taxes	−31%
All other receipts	−14%
Total Budget Receipts	−8%

2. excise taxes

3. 2008: $2.5 trillion ($2,524 billion);
   2010: $2.3 trillion ($2,332 billion)

4. −8%

5. corporation income taxes, estate and gift taxes

6. Answers will vary. Check that facts in the table support the students' conclusions. Possible conclusions: government revenues increased by almost one-third in three years; individual income taxes make up nearly half of all revenue.

Activity 15

1. Letter 1, statements of fact: The population of Lakeside is growing. Depending on how it is subdivided, this land could provide homes for ten to fifteen families. Letter 2: The land along Raccoon Lake is home to many wildflowers and animals. Every year, hundreds of hikers, birdwatchers, and other people use the land for recreation.

2. Letter 1, emotional language: desperate, have a right, wholesome sports, tree huggers, nature extremists, outrageously. Letter 2: natural beauty, future generations, ugly and barren, natural paradise, tragic loss.

3. Sample answer: The point of view of the writer of Letter 1 would be affected if he or she were a real estate agent, a builder, a person looking for a new house, or a person who enjoys boating and swimming. The point of view of the writer of Letter 2 would be affected if he or she were a nature photographer, an artist, a hiker, a birdwatcher, or a professional ecologist.

4. Sample questions for writer 1: What are your financial interests in seeing that houses are put on this land? Do you want to build a house? Do you sell boating or fishing equipment? Can you support your statement that people are desperate for housing? For writer 2: What are your hobbies? How much will taxes increase if the town purchases this land? What will the town need to spend each year to maintain this land? What percentage of the town's residents will actually benefit from a nature preserve?

Copyright © by The McGraw-Hill Companies, Inc.

Activity 16

1. S, 5

2. P

3. S, 4

4. P

5. P

6. S, 2

Activity 17

Students' answers will vary. However, they should be similar to the following responses.

1. The general purpose is to explain stocks and stockholders.

2. People who purchase stocks are known as stockholders and are part owners of a corporation.

3. **a**) Shares of stock entitle the buyer to a certain part of the future profits and assets of the corporation selling the stock.

b) As proof of ownership, the corporation issues stock certificates.

c) Stockholders, or owners of stock, benefit from stock in two ways.

d) One is through dividends, the return a stockholder receives on the amount that he or she invested in the company.

e) Some people buy stock just to speculate.

Activity 18

Students' answers should be similar to the following responses.

1. When growth in the Gross Domestic Product slowed, growth in people's disposable income slowed, too.

2. None; at times the growth of personal incomes slowed but the overall incomes did not decrease.

3. Far West; by adding the quarterly percentages

4. The United States economy was growing, although it appeared to slow down in mid-1999.

Activity 19

INFLATION

CAUSES	EFFECTS
3. Consumers, businesses and governments try to buy more goods and services than the economy can produce.	**1.** Prices go up, the dollar buys less, and people on fixed incomes have decreased purchasing power.
4. The federal government spends more money than it collects in revenues.	**2.** Interest rates go up and spending on automobiles and houses falls.
5. The cost of labor goes up forcing manufacturers to raise prices.	**6.** People speculate heavily to take advantage of rising prices.
8. Higher prices force workers to ask for higher wages.	**7.** Loans are repaid in dollars that have less purchasing power because they buy less.
9. The Federal Reserve System increases the money supply faster than the increase in the Gross Domestic product.	**8.** Higher prices force workers to ask for higher wages.
10. The cost of a raw material such as oil unexpectedly increases.	

Copyright © by The McGraw-Hill Companies, Inc.

ANSWER KEY

Activity 20

1. F

2. F

3. O

4. O

5. F

6. F

7. F

8. F

9. O

10. F

Students' opinions will vary. The following responses are examples.

Opinion 1, based on item 5: Credit is too easily obtained in this country.

Opinion 2, based on item 1: The Federal Reserve is of relatively little use in improving the economic well-being of typical Americans.

Activity 21

1. Answers may vary. Since the article is a newspaper account written soon after the statistics were released, some students may decide that it is a primary source. Since the article analyzes those statistics, some students may decide that it is a secondary source. Some students will see that it contains aspects of both primary and secondary sources.

2. stating facts

3. The writer cites the government, specifically the Commerce Department, which is a reliable source for economic statistics.

4. Sample answer: spending and inflation statistics for other times in the 1990s; employment statistics; interest rates; information on the GDP; stock market trends; contemporary economists' analysis of the economy

Activity 22

Students' explanations will vary. The following explanations are examples.

1. V Many Europeans believe that food imported from the United States is unsafe.

   The passage discusses the arguments Europeans use to avoid importing American food but does not mention that the United States uses health issues as barriers to international trade.

2. V American workers have demonstrated opposition to imported goods.

   The passage discusses how American workers oppose importing goods but does not discuss how trade barriers help save American jobs.

3. V Protectionist measures provide only temporary protection for domestic jobs.

   Although the passage discusses the disadvantages of inefficient industries, it does not mention the rewards of efficient industries.

Copyright © by The McGraw-Hill Companies, Inc.

Activity 23

1. demand-side

2. supply-side

3. demand-side

4. supply-side

5. supply-side

6. demand-side

7. supply-side

8. demand-side

9. demand-side

10. demand-side

Activity 24

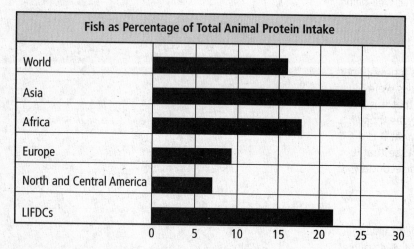

How much more than people in the world in general do people in low-income food-deficit countries depend on fish for protein? 5.4%

Copyright © by The McGraw-Hill Companies, Inc.

Critical Thinking Activities

ANSWER KEY

Activity 25

1st	2nd	3rd	4th	5th	6th	7th	8th
c	d	a	e	g	f	h	b

Activity 26

Number of Computers Per 1,000 People in Countries with the Most Personal Computers

Country Name	Number of Computers per 1,000 People
United States	570
Canada	479
United Kingdom	441
Japan	357
France	357
Germany	338

Copyright © by The McGraw-Hill Companies, Inc.